DRAW AUSTRALIAN AN

First published in the Year of th
by
Krueger Wallac

Email: wally@adam-wallace-books.com or visit
www.adam-wallace-books.com or visit
Croydon. They have the best mini-golf courses.

ABN: 31 260 817 318

ISBN: 978-0-6489737-6-8

Printed in

Cataloguing-In-Publication entry is available
From the National Library of Australia
http://catalogue.nla.gov.au

Do not nibble on or give to a baby.

This book is not a rock or scissors. Paper for the win!

Krueger Wallace
Press

CONTENTS!

Drawing is ***SOOOOOOOOOOOOOOOOOOO*** much FUN and Australian animals are ***SOOOOOOOOOOOO*** weird!

I mean, come on! A platypus is like 37 animals in one and wombats do square poop!

But that means they're fun to draw!

So then. Hands up if you think you can't draw.

I can't see. I'm a book, but if your hand is up, I have something to tell you ...

YOU'RE WRONG!

YOU CAN DRAW!!!

You just haven't been shown ways to make it easier, it hasn't been broken into simple steps with instructions that are rhyming and funny and have koalas that start as an an icy-pole! Like it does in this book!

IT'S TRUE! YUMMMMMMMMMMM!

So get a pencil, get a piece of paper, and get ready for a whole world of fun.

Most of all, don't worry about mistakes. Everyone makes them, and remember, drawing isn't meant to be a stress, it's meant to be awesome!

HOW TO DRAW A

FISHY

WOMBAT

Something smells fishy, but that's okay,

Because we're drawing a fish today.

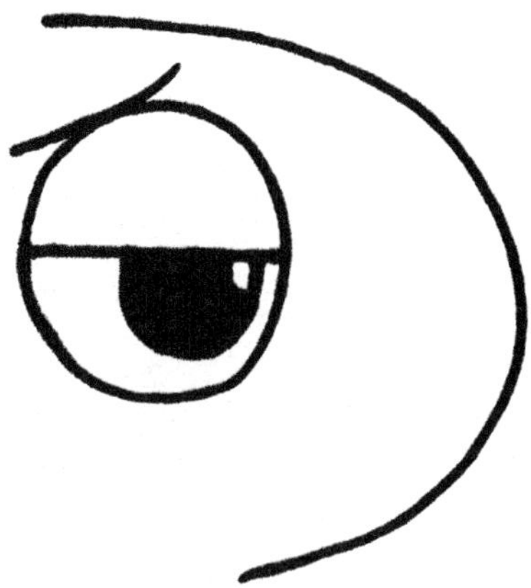

With a three second memory, your fish is a bore,

'Cos it always forgets what you just said before.

On the face do a line, and maybe a mark,

These lines will help your fish hide from a

SHARK!

He’s got bored eyes, but if you wait a short while,

He’ll forget why he’s bored and he might crack a smile.

Fish have fins, you know that they've got 'em,

But wait! These are ears, fins go down the bottom!

Finish the ears and colour the nose,

Our wombat's begun, let's see where it goes!

A right front leg, some claws on there too,

They help wombats dig, which is what wombats do.

A left front leg, for when your wombat creeps,

To steal carrots for dinner before he sleeps.

The back of the wombat curves right around,

And the back of the back's where the butt can be found.

Now a back leg, we've got two steps to go,

When wombats run, they're actually not slow!

A wombat's tummy never, ever grieves,

Because they eat vegetables, grass and leaves.

A second back leg to complete your wombat,

And you're done. Yes, you are. It's over. That's that!

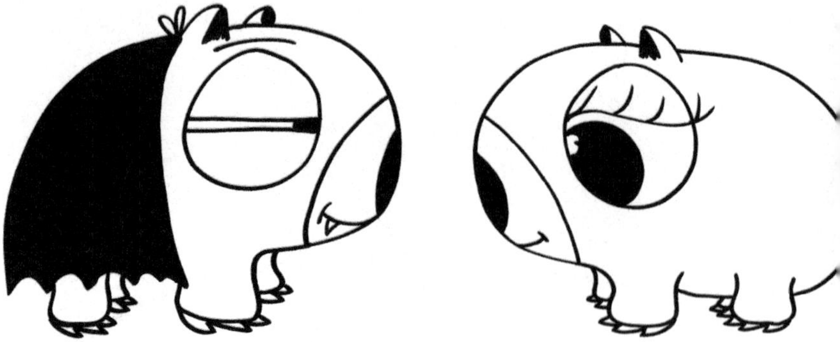

Wombats are awesome, they look kind of dopey,

But now you'll draw lots more wombats, I hopey.

HOW TO DRAW A SNOWMAN FAIRY PENGUIN

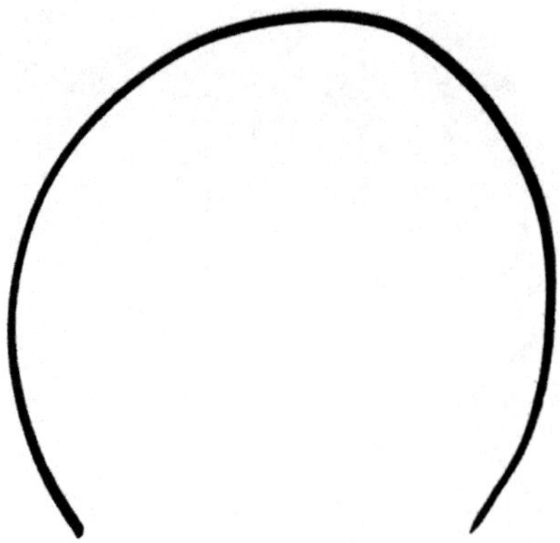

If the **SNOW** melts, your **SNOWMAN** will be dead,

So use a **SNOWBALL** to give him a head.

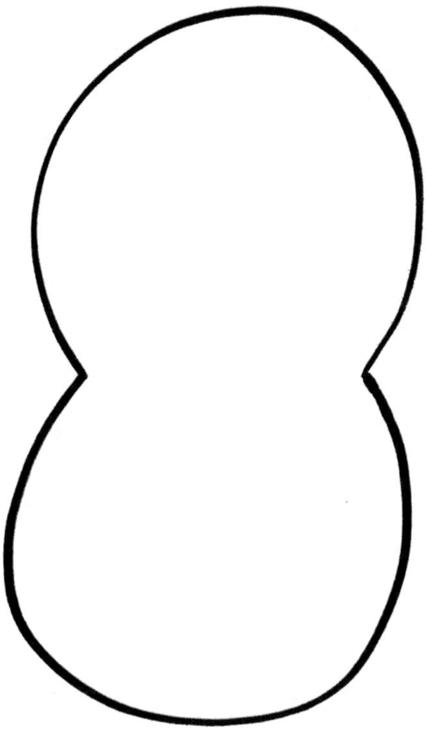

Another snowball, he's put on some weight,

Your **SNOWMAN** looks a peanut. Or, actually, an 8.

Our **SNOWMAN** is happy, at least for a while,

So now let's give him a nice big smile.

Not nearly enough! We need a bigger smile!

And then go and do something else for a while.

Now, before your **SNOWMAN** melts and dies,

Use some pebbles to give him some eyes.

Is he wearing a shirt? A jacket? A vest?

Who cares! To keep it closed, a button would be best.

BORED NOW! Our **SNOWMAN** is done,

Make his mouth a beak for some penguiny fun.

To divide up the penguin, give it a vest,

By drawing a line across its chest.

Eyes will make your penguin look bewt,

I'll try big ones. Awwwwww. Isn't he cute.

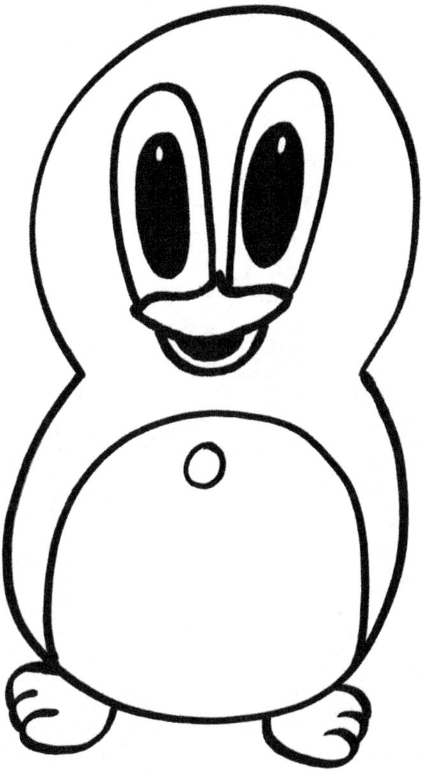

Penguins slide on their tummies for super speed,

But at waddling time, feet are what they need!

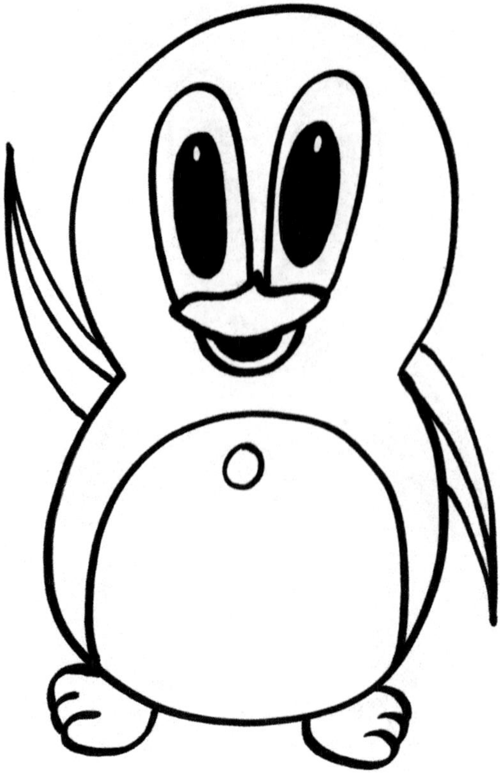

Draw wings up, down, whatever, I don't care,

Penguins can't fly so why are wings even there?

Black is worn when burglars steal loot,

But it makes penguins look like they're wearing a suit.

A bow tie for the suit, some hair up on top,

And now your penguin's done ... so **STOP!**

Penguins are awesome, we know that it's true,

Now see what different penguins ***YOU*** can do!

HOW TO DRAW A FULL MOON PLATYPUS

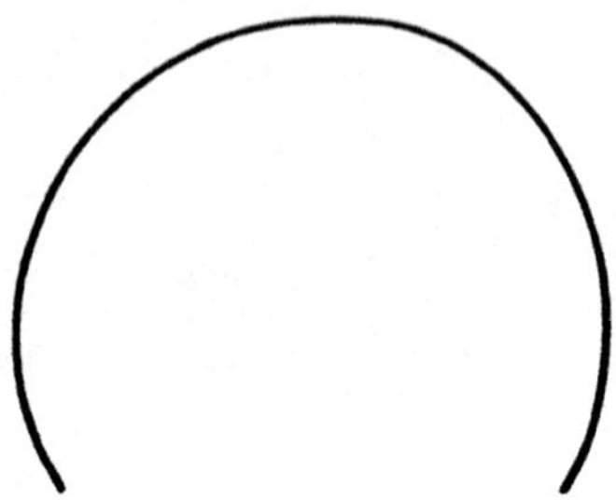

The day is done, the moon is full,

The werewolves think it's beautiful.

The moon rises over a cliff tonight,

The cliff has a slight bump, but it’s alright.

Draw another rock in the shadow of the moon,

Then **HIDE!** The wolves will be howling here soon.

To make the cliff rise up even higher,

Some mountain sides are what we require.

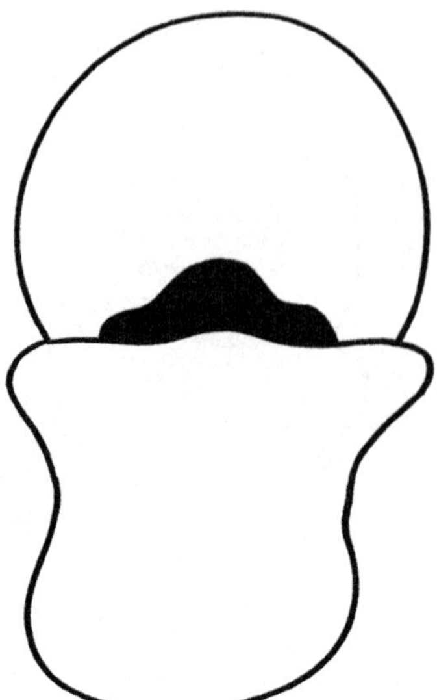

The moonlight filters down the hill,

Fortunately, it’s in the shape of a bill.

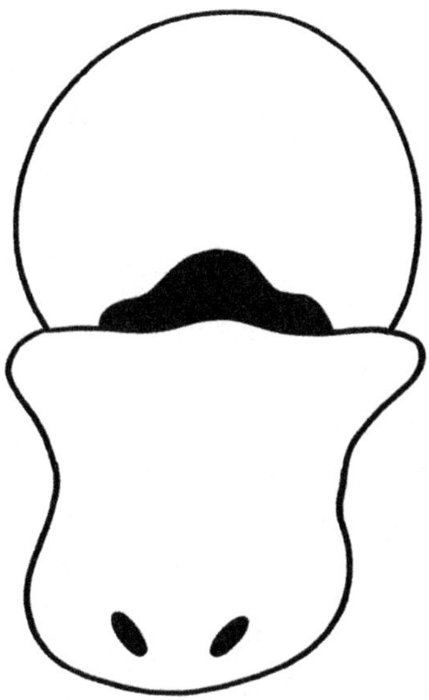

Two spots at the bottom would be the most,

Then turn it upside down to see a weird-looking ghost.

Two platypuses are called platypi,

And most of them have a left and right eye.

When swimming all day is all that you do,

I reckon that you'd have a smiley face, too.

Swimming down a river can take a while,

So this guy likes to swim freestyle.

A platypus has fur that's oily and slick,

To help keep him warm, and help keep him quick.

Now ***you*** draw the tail, don't leave it to Beaver,

YES! That's awesome! You're such a high achiever!

Some back legs for kicking, he’s not wearing slippers,

When swimming, flippers are better than slippers!

A bit of hair, then if you want it underwater,

Draw some bubbles. Yeah, I think you oughta.

Your platypus is totally fly,

But don't stop now! Draw more platypi!

HOW TO DRAW AN ICY-POLE KOALA

It's a hot summer day, the weather's fine,

Now go to the fridge 'cos it's icy-pole time!

I have to tell you that the food you've been dealt,

Is having a meltdown and is starting to melt!

You'd better move fast or your mum will shout,

Put your treat on a plate so the drips don't drip out.

It dribbles down the stick and starts to spread,

Don't get it on the carpet or you will be **DEAD!**

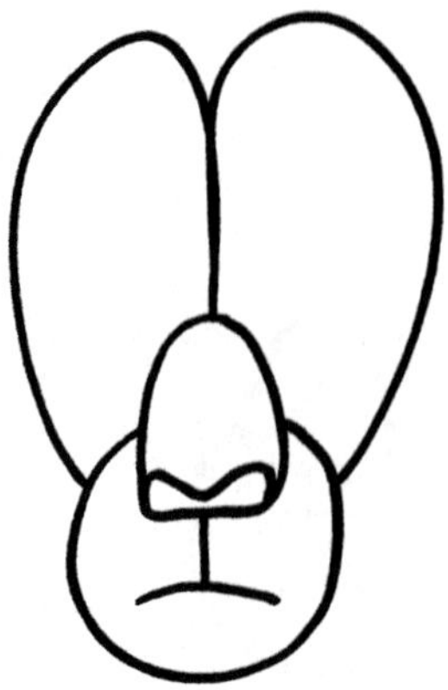

OH NO! Now the top's melted too!

There are two huuuge puddles! What will you do?

It's okay. Don't stress. Stressing's unwise,

Koalas don't stress. At least, not when they have eyes.

Two lines on the mouth aid gum leaf chewing,

And help close things up to avoid gum leaf spewing.

A circle for the head is the next thing to do,

And I suppose we should colour the nose in, too.

When koalas eat gum leaves, it makes them sleepy,

But without any ears, your koala looks creepy!

A back and a leg will help provide grip,

Then three sharp claws make sure it won't slip.

Another leg, well, I suppose it's an arm,

More claws help your koala come to no harm.

Well, it was a magic koala, just floating around,

So draw in a gum tree, which is where he'll be found.

Well done, by gum! Your koala looks great,

Now draw ***more*** koalas, so he can have a mate.

HOW TO DRAW A YO-YO ECHIDNA

Get ready, get set, it's time to go-go,

We start our echidna by drawing a yo-yo.

How long is a piece of string? I don’t know-know,

But draw some string or your yo-yo won’t go-go.

So your yo-yo works well, and not just so-so,

A loop at the end's where your finger will go-go.

Around the world is a long way to go-go,

Two sides make sure your yo-yo's not slow-slow.

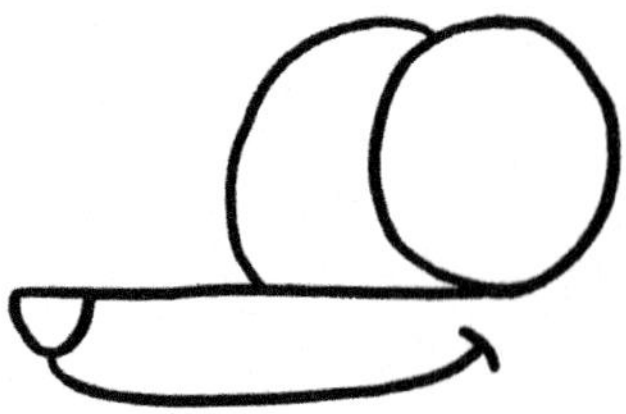

When you walk the dog, if you throw-throw,

A ball, the smile on his face will grow-grow.

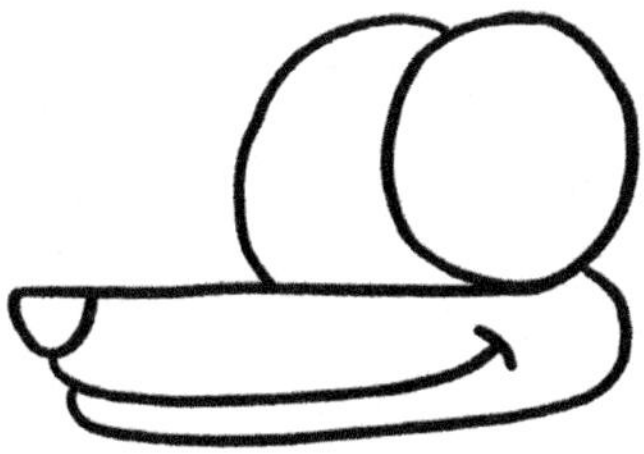

They’re extinct, so please, don’t be a dodo,

Your echidna’s chin goes down below-low.

When ants walk in a nice, straight row-row,

Echidnas lick them up. Tastes good? I don't know-know.

You're doing well, now the next thing to show-show,

Are eyeballs and eyebrows, you know where they go-go.

We don’t want to upset the status quo-quo,

But nostrils are needed to sniff-sniff and blow-blow.

Some hair goes up high-high, and then down low-low,

If it's not cut it will continue to grow-grow.

This echidna's back is as smooth as snow-snow,

If you ski it, it gets steep, so look out below-low!

In a rowboat, you have to row-row,

But when running around, don't stub your toe-toe!

To make bread, chefs have to knead the dough-dough,

But you need to draw another back leg and toe-toe!

It's good to pay back the money you owe-owe,

And to draw a front leg, from go-go to woah-woah!

You draw like an expert, a total pro-pro,

Do the chest and front leg! Quick! Don't be slow-slow!

Our bald echidna needs spikes in a row-row,

So put them all in. Ready ... Set ... Draw!

HOW TO DRAW A NIGHTY NIGHT PELICAN

It’s late at night, it’s time for bed,

Time to rest your weary head.

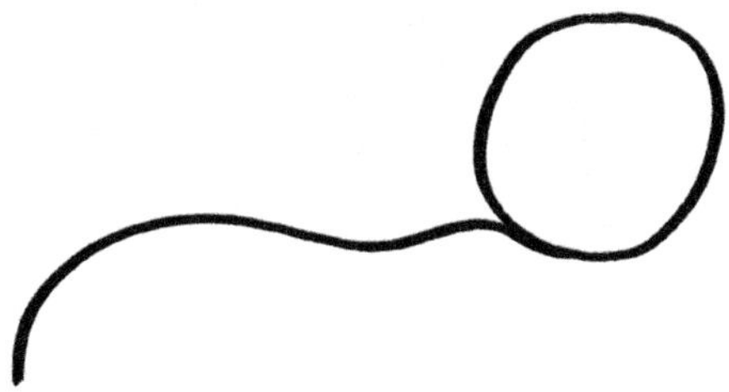

It looks like a balloon with a piece of string,

But it's not. It's a body. It's ***REALLY*** exciting.

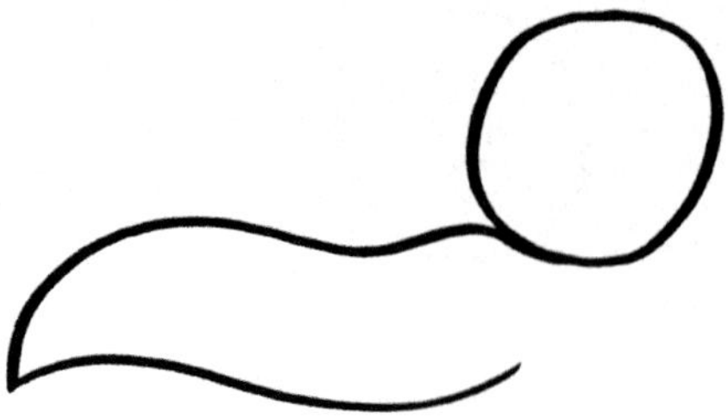

To help our friend get a good night's rest,

Draw in the mattress. Yes, that would be best.

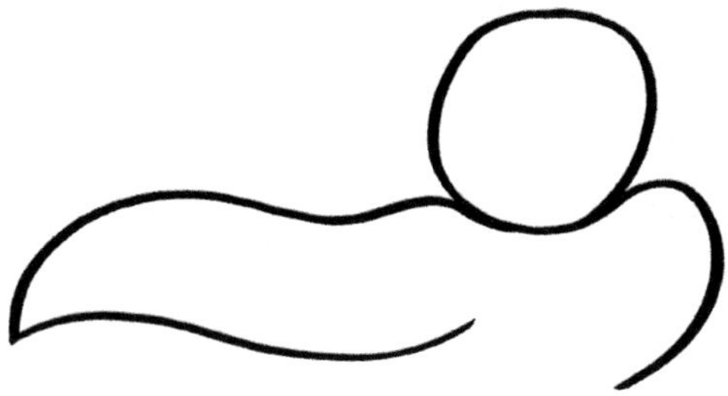

A bit of support behind his head, there you go,

A nice, mediumly firm, evenly fluffed-up pillow.

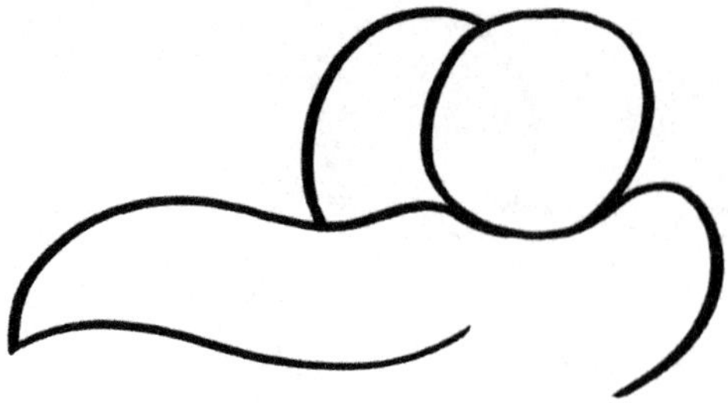

And now there's more than one person to see,

His wife's come to bed after watching TV!

Sleeping time's over! Get up and dance,

My pelican looks like a real smarty pants.

A little line lines up the end of his mouth,

And then his ***huuuuuuge*** beak hangs down south.

Start between the eyes, go on, get in there,

Then give your pelican some funky looking hair.

Okay, hang tough, you have to hold your nerve,

As we draw the neck in a nice, smooth curve.

I don't like politics, but here's the thing,

You need to draw in the pelican's left wing.

Curve around for his chest, past his butt with some bumps,

And don’t forget to draw in two little leg lumps.

Compared to lions, pelicans are tough,

Because they don't need four legs, just two is enough.

Another wing at the top, at the back a little tail,

If you draw the tail at the front, I'm afraid that's a fail.

Our pelican is looking kind of alright,

But he barracks for Collingwood! Make him black and white!

Look at that! You can draw a pelican now!

From here on ***you*** can change it … but how?

HOW TO DRAW A BALLOON KANGAROO

To start off this cartoon drawing thing,

Draw two balloons and one piece of string.

If our balloons flew away it would make us frown,

So use a weight and more string to hold them down.

More string! More string! Curl this lot around,

Then use some pegs to stick it into the ground.

Our balloons look good, but wait! ***NO! STOP!***

Spears and a cactus will make them pop!

Phew, it's okay, our balloons look fine to me,

Now draw in some eyes so our kangaroo can see!

A kangaroo's neck is atatched to its head,

If it wasn't ... well ... it would probably be dead!

Now the favourite bit for a chiropractor to crack,

It's time to draw in the kangaroo's back.

Without this our kangaroo picture would fail,

So go for it! Draw in the kangaroo's tail.

To help them accomplish every jumping feat,

Kangaroos have strong back legs and ***MASSIVE*** back feet!

Kangaroos eat grass, they thjink that it's yummy,

But it will spew out if they don't have a tummy.

And now, to add a little extra charm,

Stick on a teeny little T-Rex arm!

Your kangaroo rocks! It looks the best!

Now make it more solid by drawing a chest!

The second last step, this one is swell,

Another arm, some freckles, and speed lines as well.

It looks like our kanga is flying around,

So perhaps we'd better draw in the ground.

That's it! We've drawn an awesome kangaroo,

Now ... how many different versions can ***YOU*** do?

OTHER BOOKS BY ADAM WALLACE

THE JACKSON PAYNE ADVENTURES
(6 BOOKS!)

THE NEW YORK TIMES BESTSELLING
HOW TO CATCH SERIES
(13 BOOKS)

A VERY DINOSAUR BIRTHDAY!

HEAPS OF OTHER HOW TO DRAW
BOOKS!

THE FARTBOY SERIES
(9 BOOKS)

THE FART CLUB SERIES
(4 BOOKS)

THE FARTY PETS SERIES
(4 BOOKS)

AND MORE COMING SOON ...

ABOUT THE AUTHOR

Adam Wallace has had hair of many different colours.

Once it was purple. Once it was pink. Once it was blonde. Once it was orange. Once it was blue. Once it was a green mohawk. Once it was black. Once it was red. Once it was ... no. I think that's it.
Oh.
Once it was brown.
That was natural.

Adam is about to go and do some chin-ups ... in fact, by the time you read this he will have done them ... or he may be dying his hair.
I don't know.
It's a mystery.
Not a very exciting one.
I mean, no one died ... well, the hair may have died, or been dyed, but that's an easy whodunnit to solve.
Anyway.
Have a nice Tuesday!

Printed in Great Britain
by Amazon

41373884R00066